C000215842

THE IRON MEN OF THE ROAD

T. McTaggart

ACKNOWLEDGEMENTS

This book was only possible with the assistance, encouragement and practical help of a great many people. I am particularly indebted to Alan Duke, Les Burberry, A.J. Martin, Iwan Jones, C.G. Mileham, C. Lloyd, Steven Mustill, H. McCulloch, R.A. Whitehead, W.S. Love, F. Strange, Rory Woolf, R. West, S.P. Scholey, P.G. Smart, the late T.B. Paisley all of the Road Locomotive Society, the Mitchell Library Glasgow, the Strathclyde Archives, the Gwynedd Archives, the Museum of Transport, Glasgow, the Belfast Telegraph, the Glasgow Herald, the National Traction Engine Trust, Messrs. N. & E. Peebles, Ltd., John Young (Kelvinhaugh) Ltd., the Central Electricity Generating Board, Belfour Beattie, Ltd., Chas. Harkness, G. Howarth, Dr. J. Manners, Mrs. M. Gardner, A. Cobb, A. Mackinlay retired Pickfords manager, W. Bibby, Len Crane, the late Bob Field, Arthur Calvert, Ian Muir, Reg Colinson, the Scottish Traction Engine Society and all who helped in so many ways.

T. McTaggart
April 1989

Colour Picture on front cover supplied by:
S.P. Scholey, Millfields Cottage, Everton Hill, Everton, Doncaster, S. Yorks.

THE IRON MEN OF THE ROAD

T. McTaggart

Alloway Publishing
AYR

© T. McTaggart, 1989.

First Published in 1989
by Alloway Publishing Ltd.,
Darvel, Ayrshire.

Printed in Scotland
by Walker & Connell Ltd.,
Hastings Square, Darvel.
Ayrshire.

ISBN 0 907526 41 1

CONDITIONS OF SALE

This book is sold subject to the condition that it shall not,
by way of trade or otherwise, be lent, re-sold, hired out or
otherwise circulated without the publisher's prior consent
in any form of binding or cover other than that in which it
is published and without a similar condition including this
condition being imposed on the subsequent purchaser.

INDEX

THE IRON MEN OF THE ROAD

The Iron Men of the Road is a nostalgic look at the story of the heavy haulage firms of the British Isles.

From John Harkness of Belfast, through England and Wales into Scotland only one heavy haulage firm did not start up specifically to haul Lancashire boilers and in fact this firm was in business for sixty years without ever moving a single Lancashire boiler. This firm was the Road Steam Engine Co. of Glasgow who started in business to move marine engines and boilers to the ships and with the exception of some locomotive work, stayed with marine work.

Every other firm handled Lancashire and Cornish boilers and in fact had it not been for these boilers there would have been no need for most of the firms.

When it was first suggested writing a book on this subject it was thought that it would mainly be a collection of Fowlers with a couple of Burrell users. But strange to relate, there turned out to be wide cross section of makes with Fowlers slightly ahead, but only slightly. Even Norman E. Box had as many Garretts, as he had Fowlers plus two McLarens.

This book deals mainly with heavy haulage firms but as some big loads were moved by threshing and agricultural contractors, to fill in a quiet period in their businesses, a few of these are also included although they were not really haulage firms. No Cornish firms are included although they moved many heavy lifts as they were all part time heavy hauliers.

This book is a follow-on to "Pioneers of Heavy Haulage" and "The Big Box" by the same author.

THE IRON MEN OF THE ROAD

J. HARKNESS & CO.
Belfast

In 1961 John Young (Kelvinhaugh) Ltd., of Glasgow was asked to supply a 25 ton mobile crane to lift an economy boiler in Belfast Northern Ireland by their customer Penman & Co. Ltd., of Strathclyde Street, Glasgow as no crane of this lifting capacity was available in Belfast.

Youngs despatched the crane. A Coles mobile lorry-mounted to Preston for shipment by the only ro-ro boat operating at that time to Ulster. As they arrived in Preston, Youngs vehicle uplifted the boiler from Penman and delivered it to the Clyde Villa crane at Plantation Quay on the Clyde where it was lifted on to the Belfast bound ship.

The Coles crane was met in Belfast by J. Harkness & Co's heavy haulage foreman, Tom Brownlee, who stated that he was the 'Bubbly' Young of Ulster. (In Glasgow 'Bubbly' Young had a reputation for doing things in an unorthodox way). Tom detailed the route to the Ormaeu Bakery that had ordered the boiler.

The crane arrived in time but had to await the arrival of the boiler. Suddenly the second man said 'Do you see what I see?' As a small Garrett steam tractor came rolling around a corner with the 25 ton boiler in tow.

Brownlee explained what was required of the crane. 'First of all', he said we will lift steel plates up onto the flat roof of the two storey building. While the squad lays them, 'we will lift this articulated unit, that had just arrived onto the plated roof. Then lift the boiler off the trailer on to the ground and lift the trailer minus the forecarriage up to be coupled to the unit.

1. — Harkness of Belfast 1910 enroute from Belfast Quay to a linen mill in County Tyrone with a forty tons Lancashire boiler by Penman of Glasgow sitting on a William Kerr & Co's bogie. The bogie remained with Harkness as it was to cost too much to ship it back to Glasgow. Hauling is a 6NHP Garrett, 'Vera' No. 27946 of 1909, on unknown Aveling and a Garrett tractor.

Now we lift the boiler up to sit on the trailer. The unit will run across the roof to place the boiler in the position for lowering into the boiler house below.'

And it all worked out as he said. The winch on the Garrett was used with three and two blocks otherwise the boiler would have come down and the light tractor would have gone up.

John Harkness had been sent to Belfast as the traffic manager for Cowan & Co., of Glasgow about 1860, having previously been in the employ of a shipping company. Seeing the great potential for a carting contractor in Belfast at that time, he raised some capital, to put a few horses and carts on the road in his own name.

A number of shipping lines made regular sailings from Glasgow, Liverpool, Preston, Bristol and London. with daily turn arounds, that is:— in early, unload, reload and away again by evening. This also meant that all the cargo landed had to be distributed and the outwards cargo picked up and delivered to the ship, from agriculture and industry, promptly.

As industry grew in Ulster someone had to move the Lancashire boilers, and other fairly heavy machinery being landed for the linen mills as well as catering for two local shipyards. In 1907 a new Garrett tractor was purchased No. 26518 reg No. 01599 to be followed by another two in 1909 plus a 6NHP road locomotive 'Vera' in December No. 27946. Another nine Garretts and one Wallis & Stevens tractor joined the fleet up to 1920. Also a Fowler compound 8NHP and an Aveling road locomotive appeared in the fleet.

By the end of the first world war there were 600 horses, some motors and steamers, plus hired cartage.

In the early thirties Southern Ireland embarked on the building of a Hydro-electric power scheme at Shannon which required the installation of generators and transformers etc. As Harkness was the only heavy haulage contractor in Ireland, he was contracted to move all the heavy lifts. This meant that 'Vera' and a tractor, complete with a new trailer for the heavy lifts, were away for months on end.

Just before the second world war two second-hand Sentinel steam wagons were purchased and a few I.C. engined vehicles but the bulk of the work was still done by horses. If ever any engines had to work it was the Garretts both 'Vera' and the tractors. They were working to capacity at most times.

One job that 'Vera' had to attend to was in Harland & Wolffs shipyard when they used drag chains at a launch 'Vera' hauled lumps of them back up the slipway as no other vehicle could do—for a steam vehicle had full power from a standing start. The rivets holding the near coupling sat in elongated holes in the tender and how this held the water in, goodness knows.

In the late forties and early fifties, Scammells and Diamond T's were purchased for the heavy work

2. — J. Young & Co., crane lifting Harkness Karrier artic unit on to roof to move the boiler, 1962.

but no other vehicle could haul the slipway chains like 'Vera'. On the carrying side new Bedfords arrived to replace the horses. In the sixties it was hard to get drivers for the Garretts, most men did not want the hardship of a steam vehicle while others sat in a comfortable cab.

During the 1970's the firm was plagued with union trouble, with strikes and go-slows until the union called an official strike. When 90% of the work-force stopped but 10% who were on contract jobs carried on working, Charles Harkness the managing director was visited by a union official complete with a list of wants, Charles received the sheet, looked at it, then tore it up and handed it back, saying 'Your too late lad it's all over.'

So closed a firm that had made its mark on the social history of Northern Ireland.

3. — How most machinery arrived in Belfast — a Lancashire boiler comes ashore.

4. — Vera hauling a top heavy twin gun turret 37 tons, 18ft. high in the 1930's.

5. — A condenser from Metropolitan Vickers of Manchester being wire-roped across steel plates by 'Vera' with a Garrett tractor standing by.

6. — 01 6818 appears to have lost her number plate — Garrett tractor BJ **4384**. Winching the trailer with 'Vera'.

7. — 'Vera' winching a condenser out of factory onto piggy-backed flat trailers plus 3 feet, in the late 40's.

8. — Out she comes without the condenser being tied on. It was only the timber which was wracked on with rigging screws.

9. — 'Vera' in all her glory.

LIST OF ENGINES OWNED BY J. HARKNESS: –

New 01 599	Garrett	26518	tractor	Sept 1907
BJ 710	"	27655 (later sold to Kevin McGiven, showman)	"	May 1909
BJ 728	"	27716	"	July 1909
Vera 01 6818	"	27946 (1968 to Lambe Bromsgrove)	road loco	Dec 1909
BJ 1968	"	32042 (by 1921 to Oxford Spinning Co.)	tractor	March 1914
BJ 4195	"	33414 (1966 to Lampitt & Russell, Banbury)	"	Jan 1919
BJ 4201	"	33419 (Union cartage spool converted to show Tr. by Lambe in 1968 and sold to Wallcroft Bros. Pershore)	"	Feb 1919
BJ 4384	"	33545 (? to Lambe)	"	June 1919

LIST OF SECONDHAND ENGINES OWNED BY J. HARKNESS

		Wallis & Stevens compound		
ex Antrim Iron Ore •		2926	tractor	1907
ex Bleachers Ass. Manchester to BA 3018	Garrett	33745	"	1920
ex J. Curry & Co., Belfast to BJ 4789	"	33715 (Sold 1943 to D. Rea & Co. Antrim)	"	1919
ex N.E. Box & Co. NC2025	"	33503 (Sold 1943 to J.P. Corby, Belfast)	"	1919
ex D. Rea & Co. BJ 3996	"	33332 (Sold to Mercer & Co)?	"	1918
ex Belfast Corpn BJ 4307	"	33412 (superheated)	"	1919
ex War Dept. SZ 100	"	33348 (to Cdr. J.M. Baldock)	tractor	1918

Fowler 8NHP R loco for sale 1923 — no note of Sentinels.

10. — 54 ton Alternator coming ashore for Harbour Power Station 1948.

11. — Second 86½ tons Alternator arriving at the Power Station, hauled by 'Vera' and BJ **4384**. 1948.

12. — Garrett tractor BJ **4195** with rudder post. October 1935.

13. — Autocleave from Belfast to Toombridge, 65 feet long by 7ft 6 ins diameter, weight 25 tons. August 1946.

14. — Raising and placing a Lancashire boiler weighing 30 tons into York Street Flax Spinning Company's Mill, Belfast, built by Wilson of Glasgow. March 1953.

15. — Queen's Quay Belfast, 1959.

16. — Two Diamond Ts with 120 ton load on a fairly modern trailer on loan from Sunter of Northalerton Yorks.

17. — A Guy hauling a storage tank.

18. — BJ 4195 of Harkness, still at it in 1962 assisting to deliver Penman of Glasgow economy boiler weighing 25 tons.
Photograph from John Young & Co. (Kelvinhaugh) Ltd.

19. — Stator ex Fisher vessel at Belfast on Wynns Nicholas trailer en route for Londonderry.
Nett 150 tonnes Gross 210 tonnes.

20. — Two Diamond T's plus a third over the long drags and steep climbs.

21. — With the coming of the Diamond T's out goes 'Vera' bound for preservation in England soon to be followed by her brother tractors after 60 years service. March 1968.

22. — Transformer on a Wynns trailer en route from Belfast Quay to Londonderry ex Fisher R/O vessel weight 220 tons net, 280 tons gross. Two Diamond T's plus a third on hilly route.

23. — Garrett No. 33414 of 1918 Reg. BJ 4195. Still at it in 1956.

24. — 12 ton Section of fan ex Davidson & Co. Ltd., Sirocco Works Belfast hauled by Diamond T.

25. — Another view of the fan en route to Selby, Yorks.

SCREEN BROS, Oldbury

Started as Harper & Screen and used on general haulage originally the firm gradually moved into heavy haulage in the Midlands. Although making quite a name locally was almost unknown outside the area. The late Bob Field who drove for them takes up the history.

LIST OF ENGINES OWNED BY THEM

New Burrell	No.2345	of 1900	8NHP	crane road loco	went to W.D.
by 1907 Burrell	No.2470	of 1902	8NHP	" "	
New Reg. AB 8904 Burrell	No. 3197	of 1910	8NHP	crane road loco	to L. Crane
by 1917 Reg. AB8905 Burrell	No. 2716	of 1904	8NHP	" "	sold
by 1914 Fowler	No. 10303	of 1908	A5		sold 1921
by 1917 Reg. AB 8906 Burrell	No. 3315	of ?		tractor 46-50	scrapped

WORKING FOR SCREENS

At the beginning of 1946 an advert appeared in our local Black Country newspaper for an engine driver at Screen Bros, Oldbury. I decided to apply for the job and found myself successful in getting the appointment. There were three Screen brothers — Harry, Bert and Bill. Bill had passed away at Christmas 1945; he had been the driver so I had his task. Harry was the gaffer but he did do a bit of driving if I was away ill or on holiday. Bert, the eldest, was the odd-job man. He had driven at one time but had packed it in, so if we were out on a job he was supposed to supervise.

The firm's yard was next door to Oldbury gas works; at the back of us was E. Danks' boiler works and their rubbish tip backed onto our yard. We were on the Dudley Road in Oldbury. Just inside the yard gates was the brick-built engine shed, with an inspection pit — you walked down about five steps to get under the engine. We used to put some timbers across the pit to drop the ashpan on, then get the fire pricker in the firebox and lift the middle bar up inside on top of the others, and then back underneath to manoeuvre the remainder out.

The office came next; two rooms, general office and private office, and on the walls were photos of yesteryear's endeavours. No rubber tyres in those days, it was all cast steel wheels for loads of all descriptions, the attendant lads wearing hard hats and moustaches. Next in the yard came the coalhouse which used to have a railway truck load at a time, with about 12 or 16 tons of Best Welsh Steam for the engine, with also the occasional load of Black Hard coal for the office. We sometimes used the office coal if we ran out of Welsh. That put up a smoke screen, but with the steam coal there was very little smoke. After the coalhouse came the stores, a big place with shelves etc all round and a Tortoise stove in the middle where we used to have our meals. Then came the 'machine shop', a tumble-down, wooden, open-fronted building. But just after I went to Screens, we had a new steel and galvanised sheet open-fronted building put up in replacement. The stanchions were parts of Bailey bridges welded together. Inside the building was a big old set of shears (which we used for cutting boiler plates), a drilling machine, a saw, lathe and big electric motor and a nine foot set of rolls.

The engine I was to drive was 7hp Burrell crane locomotive 3197 (AB 8904), a double crank compound which Screen Bros had bought new in May 1910. Screens had other engines at the time. There was also a larger 3 speed crane engine — Burrell 8hp double crank compound 4039 of April 1926 (NP8361). This engine had been filled up ready for a boiler inspection when it came a sharp frost, which cracked the cylinder on the low pressure side at the slide bar end. The two back wheels were off, so we pushed it out of the way with 3197 into a corner; it

was still there when I left the firm years later. Screens tried everywhere to get another cylinder block but no luck. During the first two or three years of the war 4039 had spent a lot of its time in Brum, pulling down bomb damaged buildings.

Another engine we had was Burrell Gold Medal tractor 3315 of 1911 (originally AH068) built for East Anglian Cement Co. Ltd. It was with Screens by 1917 and re-registered AB8906 in 1921, but by the time I worked for the firm the engine was worn out and disused, so we eventually broke it up. The brothers also had a colliery at Great Wyrley near Cannock and there was another old Burrell in the yard which they had used at the pit for pumping or winding purposes. It was Burrell 2716, an 8hp road engine built in 1904 and which had started life as the first showmans road locomotive to be acquired by the well known firm of Anderton & Rowland (though invoiced to A. Anderton, Middlesbrough). It was named THE SHOWMAN. After being returned to Burrells it was resold, as an ordinary road loco, to Smith Bros (Millers) of Worksop before being acquired by Screens. That engine, too, we broke up, but saved the motion and the cylinder block (which we unsuccessfully tried on 4039).

Screens made some business in removing the pit head gear and boilers from derelict pits around the Black Country, so there was always a good store of pitch pine timbers in the yard and these came in handy for rolling big boilers on and for packing. There were also a lot of old lorry solid tyres which we used for re-tyring the engine, cutting them on the power saw and fastening them to the shed stanchion, pulling them out with the engine sufficiently straight so that we could get them in our rolls, and curve them out to fit the wheels. We then drilled and bolted the sections to the wheels. Another old item lying around was an old heat exchanger, a big square box affair with a lot of tubes in it, which I understood Danks made for the British Industries Fair at Wembley in 1926 but turned out to be a failure. The tubes were the same diameter as the Burrell's though some 4 foot longer, so we appropriated some of them for retubing. The outer plates we used for boilers etc.

Of course, after World War 2 everything was in short supply and a lot of works were changing from coal to oil, and we were busy getting old Lancashire boilers out of their houses with the Burrell, and withdrawing the flues, plating up the shells and making them suitable for use as oil tanks. Everything was riveted in those days. A lot of works had brick air raid shelters on the premises and several times we had to take the adapted Lancashire boilers and put them on top of the shelters as fuel oil tanks.

Screens were also known as Midland Boiler & Tank Works and Heavy Haulage Contractors. There were seven or eight employees — a riveting gang, and four with the Burrell. When we went to and from a job there were two of us on the engine and two rode on one of the trucks with packing, jacks, coal, chains and slings and a fire-bucket for cold days and a piece of tarpaulin to throw over themselves if it was raining. We had a B licence which only allowed us to operate a 25 mile radius, not that we didn't overstep that limit a few times! There was a Ford van with a V8 engine, used to take the riveting gang out and for boiler repairs, machine moving etc.

26. — Screen Bros. Oldbury West Midlands before becoming heavy haulage contractors.

Burrell 3197 worked well for its age, especially as it was nearly always overloaded. The firebox latterly was on its last legs and we had trouble with the stays. A firm from Wolverhampton came and did welding on the boiler with a mobile unit. They would gouge a V out around the offending stay and weld it up. We took out the fusible plug and replaced it with a tapered plug and welded round it, then drilled another hole where the crown sheet metal was thicker and tapped it out, putting the plug back. All of the tubes had ferrules in their ends and I was very often in the box with expanders. We stocked and cut gauge glasses ourselves, so there wasn't any worry about those and we had plenty of other second hand fittings — the chimney and oil pump came off the older crane engine. The only part we had to buy in my time was a new right hand bearing for the main crankshaft. It came from Garretts at Leiston about 1948. We eased the crankshaft up with a jack to get the old, cracked one out and just put the replacement in — never scraped it, just put it in as it was and we never had any trouble. But the old bearing had been a headache. We were taking a boiler to a new carpet works on the west side of Kidderminster and going up the hill on Chester Road North, the bearing started smoking, so I had to pour on cylinder oil all the way up. We had the same trouble with a 50 ton hammer block when going up Castle Hill at Dudley. We were never allowed to go through Dudley town, and the police at Brierley Hill, too, were on the mark — there, the injector didn't have to blow back. Of course, we had to have the police as escort for wide loads and on occasions when we were loading up big boilers and machines in the street. I remember one time when we had to take a boiler and machines out of a tannery in Walsall. To get into the works one passed under an archway and over a small weighbridge, probably designed for horse and cart loads, so we couldn't take the Burrell in. We

27. — Screen Bros. Burrell No. 2716 with Lancashire boiler on steel wheeled bogie and tackle wagon.

had a big steel trolley about 8 or 10 feet long with cast steel wheels about a foot wide. This we had to put boilers on in awkward places. To load the boiler we arranged suitably placed timbers and rolled the boiler up them with the rope on the hind axle of the engine. Then we had to load up in the street. We did the same to unload the boilers but used the engine's rope to steady the load as it came off the wagon.

Our main wagon was a home-made one, about 20ft long by 7ft 6in wide with four narrow rubber tyred wheels on the back and four wheels on the front. We had an assortment of drawbars; if there was a long load on we had to use a longer bar. This wagon was nearly always overloaded. Another wagon was an old well frame on four wide rubber wheels, and we also had three small wagons. If we had any loads over 30 tons we borrowed an Eagle wagon from Thompsons at Wolverhampton, which would take about 80 tons. Whilst at Thompsons we would see their Fowler crane engine 17212, now well known in preservation in Len Crane's ownership and we also saw KING CARNIVAL II, Fowler 19783, in Cunliffes yard down on Wellington Road, Handsworth in Birmingham when we travelled in that area.

During my first winter, 1946-47, we had the big freeze-up and much snow. We came down in the snow from Midland Tar Distillers at Oldbury one Saturday towards the end of January and didn't go out again with the engine until the first week of March. That journey was to take a Lancashire boiler made into a storage tank down to the HP Sauce factory at Aston. We had trouble with the trams down Villa Road as the snow was still piled along the gutters, three or four feet high. I remember about that time I went up to Marsh, Chambers timber yard at Oldbury and they sawed for me out of sycamore wood some new brake blocks for both the road wheels and the flywheel.

We did a lot of work at the different tar works, shifting vessels about to new positions and taking stills off their beds, to enable our gangs to rivet on a new patch. I recall jobs at Midland Tar at Oldbury, Majors at Wolverhampton, Key's at West Bromwich; at Nechells; Greets Green; and at Swan Village gasworks. We used to go to Copper & Alloys (now Delta) at Greets Green to shift heavy machines and change their rotary furnaces of which they had two or three. A rotary furnace is about 10 or 12ft long and 5 or 6ft diameter; Danks used to make the shells. At one end the oil-fired jets blow in and the other end is the feeding end where the scrap copper, brass etc. is inserted. When molten metal is poured out of a hole in the side of the furnace, it being revolved on rollers until the metal is ready for pouring. Screens had the job of changing these furnaces when the firebrick lining got rough. We balanced them up off the rollers by picking up one end with the Burrell's crane, packing under the middle and lowering it down, then the back end would be dealt with

similarly. Now we could roll the furnace off on packing, onto our steel bogie, and pull it outside to the big gantry crane. There, in an upright position it was relined with new firebricks.

A lot of jobs were done for Wolverhampton Metals, and for James Bridge Copper at Walsall, now IMI. At Wednesfield there were square brick furnaces and every so often they would knock in the front wall for us to get the scab out of the bottom. This consisted of lead, tin, copper, brass and firebrick and was about 12ft x 24ft weighing up to 20 or 25 tons. We had to jack up the mass and drag it out with the Burrell by blocks and back axle rope, then raise it further to push our wagon underneath and take to James Bridge Copper. Here the load was dumped on waste ground for cutting up and remelting. At Wednesfield there was a rotary furnace and by it a 20ft long brick trench, some 5ft wide and 4ft deep containing ingot moulds fixed to an endless chain. The idea was to pour the molten metal into the moving moulds and they would then drop off the other end, but something went wrong and 20 tons of metal ended up in the trench — another job for Screens. Once retrieved the scrap had to be taken to James Bridge. Another time a cast iron foundry adjoining the tar works at Oldbury had 20 tons of metal come out of the furnace onto the floor and we had to go and remove that for them.

You might ask if we ever got stuck with these heavy loads. Well, the Burrell would steam on the proverbial fag end. We always had good coal, and the double high valve was used a lot, which of course made it into nearly a twin cylinder machine instead of a compound. We only got stuck once on the road and ended up having to use the winch. That was by the Arboretum at Walsall with the boiler from the tannery mentioned earlier; it was a boiling hot day and the tar was soft and the going heavy. Those narrow tyred wheels didn't make it any better. On the same job when we nearly got into West Bromwich by the Navigation Inn we found contractors had just done a hundred yards of new tarmac and we went ploughing through it, but nothing was said as notices hadn't been put up. We also did two heavy Lancashire boilers from Moor Lane GWR goods yard at Brierley Hill. There is a nasty steep hill up to Brierley Hill which we only just managed and we had to send one of our lads on ahead to see that we could keep on going. We took one of the boilers to a new rolling mill near to Eight Locks and the other to Stourbridge Refactories, Pensnett.

Another part of our equipment was a homemade alternative jib for the Burrell with which we erected the framework and roof trusses of new buildings. It was about 36ft in length. Some places we went to we had to take the engine's cab off, or drop the jib to get into the works. The cab we left suspended from the roof structure of our engine house back at Oldbury and we'd travel without it — not very nice when it

29. — Screen Bros. handling a tank.

30. — Screen Bros. erecting a storage tank that started life as a Cornish boiler.

31. — Screen Bros. with 50 ton Dyson trailer loaded with generator approximately 40 tons.

32. — Screen Bros. en route with a Lancashire boiler.

33. — Screen Bros. parked for lunch.

34. — ex Screen Bros. preserved by Len Crane.

rained. I know we were a bit of a headache to other road users when we had to stop to drop the jib and negotiate low bridges. The worst one was in Halesowen Street in Oldbury, where the GWR goods train ran down the short branch from Langley Green to Oldbury goods yard. Getting under there we sometimes used to bring the town to a halt.

A lot of ingots were moved by us to Langley Forge, 36 ton ones from Oldbury goods yard and 16 tonners from Langley Green station. The latter's crane was only a 20 ton machine but the ingots were soon moved onto our wagon, so we shifted a fair tonnage.

We also did six hammer blocks from Langley Green to a stamping works half way down Powke Lane, a steep hill going out of Blackheath. We used the old well wagon and since the blocks were only about 12 tons we did two at a time. The well wagon was utilised because it was suitably low and we could push the blocks off onto packing with the Burrell. Now the braking system on the wagon was only wooden blocks worked via two screws at the back. Wasn't there a pantomime going down that hill I had to do most of the braking with the Burrell, in low gear of course, with both road wheel and flywheel brakes hard on and the reversing gear back. Mercifully it was the only time I used that well wagon. One of the bogies from it was pressed into service to retrieve THE GRIFFIN from Longbridge.

Another hair raising job was at the Birmingham Battery at Selly Oak (we did a lot of jobs there). A big Lancashire boiler in a house on some waste ground on the other side of the canal to the main works needing moving. We were to exchange it with the works' existing boiler which involved crossing a very narrow and hump backed bridge. In the centre you could see the last layer of brickwork to the arch. We did it OK, but that was the only job on which we ever got any danger money.

About 1948 we had a job at Bloxwich Furnaces where there was a row of about six Lancashire boilers, previously fired on the waste heat from the furnaces. Close by was a big beam engine which I think pumped the air for the blast furnaces. We got out two of the best boilers and took them to our yard, then with the flues out made them into oil tanks. When the trams finished running in Birmingham, to be replaced with motor buses, there was a requirement for fuel tanks at the various bus garages. We moved several new 30ft by 10ft welded tanks from Thompsons at Bilston to different garages and installed them. Also shifted were big galvanising vats from Thompsons to different local galvanising firms. Two Cochran vertical boilers went into a trailer works at Stirchley, Birmingham. These had been brought down from Scotland to our Oldbury yard and we took them on and erected them - of course, we had to stand them upright.

Another headache was taking a 20ft diameter still from Midland Tar at Oldbury to Ratcliffes at Great Bridge to have a new bottom put in it. We notified the police in Oldbury, and loaded it up in the works yard but on arriving for work next morning we waited in vain for our escort. We ran out to the police station, to be told we should have to manage on our own, so we had no escort. On another occasion we did a wide load from Walsall to our yard with the Walsall police attending us to their boundary with West Bromwich, but here again we were left to finish the trip alone. On less glamorous jobs we have pulled lorries out of tips, and excavators which have got bogged down on building sites. We went to Bromford Lane claypit two or three times to lower their excavator down into the pit on our rope or to assist it coming back up at the end of its stint. We did a lot of work next door to our own yard at Danks Boilers, moving boilers out of the works into the stockyard or taking them out and loading them for the railway company. Danks still had their old Burrell single crank crane engine 1497 of 1890 at that time. I seem to remember it as a straight jib crane, and it had got a good collection of those little county licence plaques on it.

Other firms we did work for (a large number of them regrettably now extinct) were incandescent Heat, Smethwick; Albion Bottle; TI Accles & Pollock; Birmid, Smethwick; Birmetals, Woodgate; Hopes Windows; Mills Foundry, West Bromwich; Thomas Dudley's foundry at Dudley; Sankeys, Bilston; and lots of chain and anchor works at Cradley. We took two Lancashire boilers made into storage tanks across to a stamping works at Foleshill, Coventry and stood them on end, and two more to a pork pie factory at Burton-on-Trent, and Ind Coope's brewery. A couple of boilers put into a hospital at Worcester were delivered by Pickfords, the first brought down by their Fowler JIX. But they used an ex WD Diamond T to bring the second.

Screens also purchased a lot of secondhand vertical boilers of 10 or 12 feet in height. These had been condemned by the boiler inspector, but they were repairable and we welded them up, gave them a hydraulic test and sold them to pig farmers for gently steaming swill etc. That was a nice easy job out in the country for the Burrell. To get water in the built-up areas we had a hydrant key; we used to flood the pit and suck the water out of the hole even though it was against rules. We never got caught and kept a sharp eye out for the water company man!

Our wages were about £4 per week in 1946, rising to £6. 10s in 1950. At some places we did quite well for tips. I think the biggest tip we had was from a scrap dealer in Wednesfield, who bought five transformers from a power station at Wolverhampton. We had to empty out the oil and take them to his scrap yard. Being nearly all copper, I guess he made a bob or two. We had to negotiate our own wages and conditions with Harry Screen. No wet weather clothes were provided in those days and he was a hard taskmaster. One instance I recall was in November 1948 when we did a lot of work for Lench's of Blackheath. They had a new cold heading machine arrived from America in a crate and we had to go up there to lift it from the packing and install it in the works. I went to our yard early and got up steam, but it was pouring with rain, so we didn't set off. Harry always came down to work about 9.00 a.m. and when he found us sitting round the stove in the stores having a leisurely breakfast he wanted to know what our game was. When we said it was too wet to go up to Blackheath because the crated machine couldn't be opened in the rain, he told us to b—— off home. Next day we sat in the stores until Harry arrived and asked him if he was paying us for the previous day when he sent us home. Well, he said, we didn't work, so we wouldn't get paid. So as we knew Lench's had been anxiously phoning him up about us getting on with the job, we told Harry that we would take another day off right now. He soon altered his tone and we did get paid; he never did the same trick again.

The rope on the Burrell's crane had to be inspected by the insurance people but the long rope on the winch didn't When it got into a bad condition, which happened often owing to the rough jobs, we had to go to Danks tip and swop it for one of Danks scrap ones from their overhead cranes. They still had plenty of life for our purposes. We used the old oil lamps a few times which was just about alright with the street lights too, but it was necessary to keep opening the firehole door to see the water gauge.

And so in the autumn of 1950 came an opportunity to take a job at Averys, weighing machine manufacturers, driving their steam loco cranes. I nearly doubled the £6. 10s wages I was getting at Screens but the work was harder and in some ways it was like being a prisoner after the please yourself attitude at Screens. But I can still keep in touch with old times for I visit Len Crane a lot, and see 'my' old Burrell, now in his ownership, as well as Thompsons crane engine.

42. — W. Carter of Manchester Fowler 8NHP No. 5749 tracing his 8NHP McLaren No. 132 with a 35 ton Lancashire boiler from R. Taylor & Sons of Marsden to Bury, Lancs.

66. — Showman Jack Rose of Kingston-on-Thames. 7NHP compound Foster No. 3642 of 1908 with a captured house boat during the first world war. This engine still owned by the same family trading as Rose Brothers of Chertsey, Surrey.

86. - Frank Morgan & Co. with two 45 ton pre-war Scammells and 120 ton trailer and 100 ton transformer.

ALLAN KNIGHT,
Engineers and Boiler Makers, Huddersfield

Although they were primarily engineers, they operated several road locomotives on heavy haulage for other industries and also dealt in buying and selling engines.

The firm mainly operated McLaren road locomotives starting with No. 776 of 1906 10 NHP then:—

McLaren	No. 1528	of 1917	8NHP	CX 7903	from 1919 to 38
McLaren	No. 775	of 1905	10NHP	WR 6663	from 1921 to 25
McLaren	No. 956	of 1907	10NHP	WR7390	from 1934 to 43
McLaren	No. 731	of 1901	10NHP	YG 674	from 1932 to 34
Aveling & Porter on Boulton wheels				WR 6664	from 1921 to 24

Also purchased from H. Bentley & Co. (Bradford) Ltd., in 1945:—

Fowler	No. 9495	of 1904	B5	AK9024	ex W. Dept
McLaren	No. 1571	of 1919		NC 2305	ex S/H in 1922
McLaren	No. 1716	of 1923		WT 242	S/H in 1942

H. Bentley (Bradford) Ltd., also owned an Aveling & Porter No. 8989, bought new 1919 AK 9016 of which there is now no trace.

39. — Allen Knight of Huddersfield. Engineers and heavy haulage contractors.
One of their McLarens with a steam engine on two steel wheeled bogies.

36. — H. Bentley Fowler No. 9495 Reg. No. AK 9024 with Lancashire boiler, tackle wagon and living van.

37. — H. Bentley Fowler No. 9495 with another Lancashire boiler on a rubber tyred trailer.

POWER PLANT CO.
West Drayton

The company owned only this Clayton Shuttleworth 6NHP No. 45997 of 1913 MD 5151 purchased second hand in 1921 from G.W. Almond of Burnham, Bucks a brick maker and used to transport their heavy lifts for **their own business.**

45. — Power Plant Co. Ltd., Clayton road locomotive at West Drayton Station, Middlesex, 1926.

SOUTHERN TRANSPORT CO. LTD.
Brighton, Sussex

The company was mainly a general haulage contractor running numerous wagons and using four tractors on heavy lifts.

Second hand	1914	BJ. 2311	No. 27237	Garrett of 1908	3 ton single sold 1915
New	1914	BJ 2329	No. 32622	Garrett Tractor	sold 1925
New	1917	DX 1822	No. 27234	Ransomes Sims & Jeffries	Tractor sold 1919
Second hand	**1922**	**KE 3384**	**No. 13468**	**Fowler R3**	

49. — Southern Transport Co. Ltd., of Brighton with over worked Garrett tractor No. 32622 Reg. BJ 3239 with 30 tons Lancashire boiler.

50. – Southern Transport Garrett tractor No. 32622 with condensor.

T.W. WARD LTD.
Machinery Merchants, Silvertown, London E.

Mostly their own boilers were hauled and erected by their own men. Their main engine being overworked Garrett tractors and one Aveling Porter 3 ton tractor.

Second hand in	1905	LN 9851	No. 5672	Aveling Porter	of 1905
New	1914	BJ 1943	No. 32084	Garrett	tractor
New	1915	BJ 2558	No. 32740	Garrett	tractor
New	1924	AN 6714	No. 34410	Garrett	tractor
New	1927	AN 8301	No. 34787	Garrett	tractor

52. – Ward being assisted by first War, Commer on solid rubber tyres up a hill.

38

51. – Thos. W. Ward Ltd., Silvertown, London E. with a hard worked Garrett tractor No. 32740 Reg. No. BJ 2558 on woodblock wheels with economy boiler approximately 25 tons in the 20's.

53. - Ward nearly at the top using the winch wire.

54. — Ward at journeys end, ready to unload the boiler.

WYNN OF NEWPORT

Thomas Wynn left the railway company to put two horses with a cart on the road to deliver goods to and from the local railway goods station in 1863. Thomas died in 1878 but the firm continued to expand through peace and war with sons, grandsons and great grandsons working in the business and growing to a stable of 150 horses before the first steam vehicle arrived in 1905.

STEAM HEAVY HAULAGE VEHICLES

New	Wallis Stevens	No. 2846 of 1905	4½ ton	tractor		
New	Burrell	No. 2842 of 1906	5 ton	tractor	Reg. AX 183	sold 1913
New	Garrett	No. 28733 of 1910	5 ton	tractor	Reg. BJ 1103	sold 1921
New	Burrell	No. 3480 of 1913	6 NHP	DCC	Reg. DW 2286	sold 1923
New	Burrell	No. 3703 of 1915	6 NHP	DCC	Reg. DW 2120	sold 1923
Second hand	1919 Burrell	No. 2724 of 1905	8 NHP	DCC		sold 1920
New	Fowler	No. 15463 of 1920	rating A9		Reg. DW 2121	still owned
Second hand	1921 Garrett	No. 32703 of 1915	5 ton	tractor		
Second hand	1930 Garrett	No. 33648 of 1919	5 ton	tractor	Reg. DW 6887	

They also owned many steam wagons. Their heavy haulage went on to haul heavy lifts in Europe, Africa and Australia.

64. – John Thompson of Wolverhampton B6 Fowler No. 19783 Reg. No. EF 4883 new April 1932 'King Carnival' with a Cornish type boiler on a Dyson tank transporter trailer ex MOD.

J. HICKEY & SONS,
Richmond, Surrey – Later Cheshunt Herts

J. Hickey & Sons were engineers, boilermakers and machinery dealers (which included traction engines) also heavy haulage and machinery movers. Started in 1881 using horse haulage and later road engines, they would take on any job that was possible with their plant, moving barges, boilers, kilns, tanks, gas works equipment as well as goods for export.

LIST OF STEAM ENGINES

By 1919 ex E.T. Padfield of Shepton Mallett Burrell No. 3489 of 1913 6 NHP DCC Reg. PB 9624 in 1921 named "City of London" and sold 1936 to Swales Bolesworth a showman who travelled East London and Essex. Now with Jack Wharton.

By late 1920 ex T & W.J. Hooper of Lisheard Burrell No. 3929 of 1920 6 NHP DCC crane Reg. PB 9687 in 1921 "His Majesty". Sold in 1964 to L.J. Searle of Horsham whose family still owns it.

? ex Charles Hart of Barking Burrell No. 2011 of 1897, 8 NHP SCC Reg. No. 251 "Emperor II".

By 1925 ex J.W. Harris & Son of Hook Norton Oxon. Burrell No. 2701 of 1904 8 NHP DCC Reg. PE 8171 "Black Prince". Now at Bressingham.

By 1914 ? Clayton Shuttleworth No. unknown, sold 1916.

67. – James Hickey & Sons, Richmond. Boiler makers, engineers and heavy haulage contractors in the London area. One horse power with machinery on iron wheeled cart.

68. — J. Hickey with a compound Clayton & Shuttleworth road locomotive "Goliath" hauling an economy boiler in 1918.

69. — J. Hickey 8NHP Burrell road locomotive No. 2701 "Black Prince" Reg. No. PE 8171 of 1904 in Hammersmith London in late 1920's.

70. – J. Hickey 6NHP Burrell road locomotive No. 3489 "City of London" Reg. No. PB 9624 of 1913.

65. – Wilkinson of Leith with B5 Fowler crane No. 8920 new April 1901 with small Fowler behind trailer of lifting tackle.

185. – John Young & Co., erecting the mast on tugboat "Seiont" before launching into Loch Lomond to join its sister tug "Dart" 1946 to haul barges of sand and gravel to the Loch Sloy scheme.

186. – Liverpool in the 1920's before the tunnel when the vehicles sailed across the Mersey. No heavy haulage here.

WALTER DENTON & Co.,
Hyde, Cheshire

Despite having been in contact with a number of transport workers in the greater Manchester area I cannot find anyone who knows the history of the origins of this firm. Frank Morgan formerly Manchester depot manager of N.E. Box who had started a clearing house in the area is believed to have bought the firm over after the death of Mr. Denton. This could have been in the fifties as Frank Morgan never registered any steam vehicles.

The firm came into being in 1904 when three engines were purchased. The biggest customer was Adamson of Hyde, boiler and tank makers.

LIST OF STEAM VEHICLES

ex Tinker Shenton of Hyde	Fowler B5	No. 9015	of 1901	Edith	owned March 1904

(Reg. MA 5583 in 1921 — Scrapper 1936

unknown engine "Sally" owned June 1904?

ex Barnsley Co-op Socy.	Fowler B?	No. 4829	of 1884	owned Sept. 1904	sold 1906
ex Tinker Shenton 8NHP Compound	Aveling Porter	No. 3517	of 1895	owned 1905	by 1921 with Oliver & Morris of Margate
ex J. McNab of Hyde, dealer	Aveling Porter	No. 4024	of 1897 8 NHP single	owned 1906	sold 1914

new to J. Hardcastle & Co. Bolton. (to J & E Ison of Ashby de la Zouche)

ex C & H Crichton, Liverpool	Straker	5 Wagon	M 725	owned 1911	

unknown Burrell for sale 1918

unknown Garrett tractor for sale 1920

ex Anderson Sons & Hedley Newcastle upon Tyne	Aveling Porter	No. 6005	of 1906	6 NHP compound owned by 1920

Reg. MA 5584 by 1921 last licensed, 1932 scrapped.

ex Birmingham Pitwood Ass.	Aveling Porter	No. 9022	of 1919	7 NHP compound

owned by 1920, Reg. MA 5585, last licensed 1938

ex Gartside's Brewery, Manchester	Clayton & Shuttle-worth	No. 47132	5 ton Wagon	Reg. FE 1575	
ex Pickfords	Fowler	No. 14115	of 1914 B6	Reg. XC 9653	owned 1932
ex E. Box Ltd.	Fowler	No. 10318	of 1905 B6	Reg. WR 6790	owned 1948

Both sold 1974 to Baldwin of Augton

ex W. Storrs & Sons & Co. Stalybridge	Foden	No. 12156	tractor	converted	ex 6 ton wagon

Reg. TU 1085

?	Foden	No. 12908	tractor	on pneumatics	Reg. TE 3128

DIESELS

1939	Foden	50 ton	with winch	Gardner engine
Wartime	Scammells (3)	45 ton		Gardner engine
Post War	Scammell	25 ton		Gardner engine
	Scammell	50 ton Mountaineer		

The author can find no confirmation of the Frank Morgan involvement, Walter Denton died around the beginning of the 2nd world war and the firm was operated by his nephew Mr. Simpson.

74. — Walter Denton of Hyde Cheshire, Fowler B6 No. 14115 Reg. No. XC 9653 with a 30 ton Lancashire boiler made by Daniel Adamsons of Dukinfield Cheshire. 1930's.

75. — W. Denton Foden tractor converted from a 6 ton wagon No. 12156 Reg. No. TU 1085 with a small storage tank. 1938.

76. — W. Denton with 30ft long tank en route to Glasgow on traction engine trailer. 1930's.

77. — W. Denton Foden diesel tractor 50 tons with 45 ton boiler from Dudley to Glasgow 1939.

78. — W. Denton 45 ton Scammell articulated Reg. No. HMA 321 war time built. With 50 ton transformer in late 40's.

79. — W. Denton 20 ton Scammell articulated Reg. No. LMA 644, late 40's.

80. — W. Denton with a new breed of Scammell the Mountaineer 50 ton tractor with a Lancashire boiler in the 50's.

81. — W. Denton Mountaineer with a tank.

53

82. — W. Denton Mountaineer with export load.

83. — W. Denton Fowler September 1937, No. 14115, B6 of 1914 Reg. No. XC 9653 purchased from Pickfords 1932.

84. – W. Denton Fowler No. 10318 of 1905, B6, Reg. No. WR 6790 waiting for a job that never came. 1960's.

85. – W. Denton journeys end in 1974 sold to C. Baldwin of Augton. Fowler No. 10318 and Fowler No. 14115 Sunny Boy No. 2'' without a rear coupling.

H. & W.E. HUGHES & SONS, Llanwrst, North Wales

H. & W.E. Hughes & Sons was mainly a general and heavy haulage contractor who sub-contracted for Norman E. Box. Hughes crews were more experienced in coping with the mountainous terrain of the Welsh valleys.

130. — H & W.E. Hughes & Sons Burrell single crank compound road locomotive No. 1667 of 1893 purchased from Girling & Co., Ipswich 1907. Hauling ex Manchester Ship Canal, Manning Wardle 0-6-0 locomotive to Hydro Scheme at Dolganrog.

131. — H & W.E. Hughes & Son Burrell No. 2811 hauling four trucks for Hydro scheme at Dolganrog.

MARSTON ROAD SERVICES, LTD., M.R.S. Ltd.
Lightbody Street, Liverpool

Marston operated two Fowlers — B6 crane road locomotive No. 17106 of 1928, KD 2826 with cylinder sizes of 7″ x 12″ and with a 12″ stroke – a super Lion. The second a DN class 5 NHP Hercules Tractor No. 17293 of 1928, UA 2464, as well as a few Sentinels, a Robey overtype wagon and about forty petrol wagons -- Mainly Scammell 15 and 25 tonners and some AEC's.

In 1926 another heavy haulage firm came up for sale after the death of the owner Edward Box father of Norman E. Box the well known Manchester heavy haulier known as "The Big Box." Edward died in 1925 leaving his widow and foreman to run the business. Although Norman was asked to take over the business, he refused as he did not get on with his stepmother his own mother having died when he was very young.

Chas. Gray of Neston, Wirral, valued the business then purchased Fowler No. 7963 and a Marshall Fowler 9983 was bought by J. Routledge of Liverpool and the remainder including the Box name and good will, various trailers and Avelins & Porter KND tractor 8927 (Nc 2029) went to Marston.

When the two Fowlers next appeared they had the caption "In Association with E. Box" printed on the engine sidecovers.

In 1928 Marston ordered a 100 ton Scammell articulated vehicle. The reader must appreciate that Scammell Lorries Ltd., of Watford had only started building vehicles in 1920 copying the American Blaw Knox machine which were first seen in this country during the first world war. The 45 tonner had only appeared succeeding the 25 tonner, which appeared after the 15 tonner. All those vehicles were articulated and now here was a young firm being asked to build the worlds largest lorry.

In November 1929 the vehicle KD 9168 was delivered to Liverpool. It was fitted with an 80 BHP petrol engine. Scammells other smaller articulateds and rigid six wheelers were driven by the same engine. This example on the 100 tonner was geared down to a transfer box at the back-end which had a speed change gear in front of the sprocket wheels that formed the final drive to the rear wheels of the tractor. Two speeds were provided, one for pulling a load and the other for empty running. There were two axles in line of the oscillating type, with chain drive to each wheel. Four wheels in line on the two axles.

The normal amount of petrol consumed on a hard, fairly level road was one gallon per mile, but on a heavy road it was two or three gallons per mile — that is without a tracing vehicle.

Two trailers arrived with the prime mover, both with swan necks. Under the swan neck was a turntable that was superimposed on another turntable, at the rear of the tractor. This of course, made it an articulated vehicle but just before road fund taxing Marston had two jocky wheels fitted inside the main beams this making it into a normal trailer that could be pulled without coupling up to the turntable. By

87, — Marston Road Services of Liverpool. Fowler B6 No. 17106 KD 2826 with 38 ton Lancashire boiler. This engine has larger cylinders than any other B6 used by heavy hauliers NHP rating over 11NHP equal only to John Thompsons Fowler and slightly below Kerrs, Burrell "Clyde".

88. — MRS Ltd., Fowler No. 17106 while hauling a 70 ton marine boiler 1929. Kicked off the road it even happened to the best of them.

this ploy MRS could license the tractor of the outfit as a heavy haulage locomotive at about a third of the cost of an articulateds license.

One of the trailers had rails set into the trailer bed to suit various gauges of railway locomotives built at the Vulcan Foundry and other locomotive builders in the Manchester area. At the rear the trailers had two rows of four double wheels on oscillating axles. The wheels were fitted with brakes and the rear axle was steered by a ships type wheel fitted behind the axles, later to have a small cabin to protect the steerer from the weather. A telephone link was provided to advise the back steerer what was required of him.

The second trailer was much shorter but had the same amount of wheels. Both had hydraulic swan-necks that could be raised or lowered to suit bridges etc. Originally operated by hand pump, a single cylinder petrol engine. (second hand from a three wheeler van) was later used to power the pump.

Three of the one hundred ton Scammells were built at the same time. The second disappeared to South America, never to be heard of again. However the third had an interesting history. It was registered BLH 21 for a tin mining company in Cornwall and Garratts of Leiston built the crusher and screen which was mounted on its trailer. This tractor later turned up at Pickfords Manchester depot.

In 1931 a Gardner engine was fitted in the MRS 100 tonner, giving a much higher return per gallon of fuel.

E.C. Marston, although handicapped by having one leg, spent a lot of time travelling about the country to see both existing and prospective customers. He operated under the titles of E.C. Marston, Ltd., MRS Ltd., and Marston Road Services Ltd. Most of the vehicles were Scammells and the AEC's on hire purchase, with a few Sentinels, the Fowler steamers and the Robey wagon. By 1933 the firms were in a bad way financially owing to over commitment and taking on cheap traffic for the sugar industry.

It may seem an act of providence therefore when the Lightbody Street depot in Liverpool went on fire, burning all the AEC's and other loss making vehicles but saving the 100 tonner, Fowler 17106 (although its rear tyres were burnt off) and a Ford service van. Of course, being a long distance firm, a few Scammells were not at home at the time.

Edward Box & Co. Ltd., Speke Hall Road, Liverpool 19

The Marston business was reformed as Edward Box & Co. Ltd., under Colonel Hudson, who had earlier financed E.C. Marston. One of the conditions imposed was that E.C. Marston retired from the business. A brand new depot was opened in Speke Hall Road. The few 25 ton Scammells left had 45 ton backends and 6LW Gardner engines fitted and with a fresh coat of paint these were like new.

89. — MRS Ltd., Fowler No. **17106** en route to Glasgow with railway coach for shipment. Home built trailer with Sentinel DG6 rear bogies.

90. — MRS Ltd., 20 ton Scammell on how not to descend a Glasgow street that local drivers managed to avoid.

91. — MRS Ltd., 100 ton Scemmell of 1929 KD 9168 with a whale for Morecambe. 75 tons.

92. — MRS Ltd., on arrival to a Mayors welcome.

As the Edward Box name re-appeared on the roads on the Fowler and the Scammells, Messrs. Pickford of Manchester served a writ against the use of the Box name, but they were unsuccessful despite a battle in the courts.

The new Edward Box firm moved forward in leaps and bounds, adding vehicles for work in London including a Garrett undertype tipper and shunting vehicles. A Scammell ran from Bradford to London on night trunk, a service called the London Textile Express. Bedford and Morris five tonners ran fish from Milford Haven to London's Billingsgate market. About fifty lorries were in service in 1937 mostly Scammells. The firm also had a depot in Birmingham.

The 100 tonner with its new diesel engine was now producing a one to three hundred per cent increase in mileage over the petrol engine. On occasion it was 5 MPG, but usually 2 or 3 and of course the fuel was much cheaper than petrol.

In pre-war days the firms heavy haulage fleet at Liverpool was:—

Fowler	17106	KD 2826	with crane	Class B6
Fowler	17293	UA 2464	5 NHP	Class DN
Scammell Artic low loader	24ft 6ins well	45 ton max load		
Scammell Artic low loader	12ft 6ins well	67 ton max load		
Scammell artic	6 wheel cable float	petrol	12 tons	
2 Scammell	Drawbar tractors	Gardner	6LW	no winch
1 Scammell	Drawbar tractor	Petrol engine		no winch and the trailers

Double crank framed low loader to carry 100 tons (bogies off Eagle 50 tonner)
Eagle 50 ton trailer (fitted with Sentinel DG solid tyred bogies) to carry 80 tons
40 foot pole wagon 40 tons (Sentinel DG bogies at rear, Scammell rear wheels on front)
Scammell drop frame, four in line front and rear on solids to carry 40 tons
Scammell drop frame, four in line at rear on solids to carry 25 tons
Scotch bogie, four wheels on solids, to carry 20 tons
Sentinel 10 tons platform on solids ex Mifie & Co., Sugar refiners
Carrimore 10 tons platform on solids ex Commercial Motor Show
Coal trailer on solids for engine.
Living van, broken up 1936/37

93. — MRS Ltd., 100 tonner at Barking Power Station.

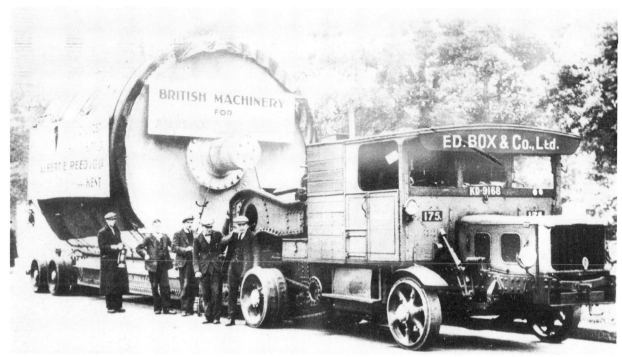

94. – MRS/E. Box & Co. Ltd., 100 tonner leaving Bury for Aylesford Kent with 14ft 1in diameter paper roll weighing 60 tons.

95. — E. Box pre-war Pioneer Scammell second-hand from the Newcastle Electric Co., in wartime rig with home built trailer again on Sentinel DG6 bogies.

96. — E. Box with three ex-army Scammell tank transporters hauling a large transformer from Metro-Vickers of Manchester.

97. — E. Box 100 tonner entering the eye of a needle.

98. — E. Box 100 tonner with large rudder canted on trailer.

From 1938 onwards there were added a new 45 ton Scammell unit with home made trailer to carry 60 tons; one 15 ton Scammell artic and two rigid six wheelers with Gardner 4LW engines.

We now come to the World War 2 period. In 1940 a second hand Fowler arrived No. 10318 WR 6790 a 1905 built B6 from a showman W.H. Marshall of Bradford. Later, a pair of six wheel pioneer Scammells were purchased from the Newcastle Water Board. These vehicles were rebuilt as heavy haulage tractors. Two more followed from the Army plus a four wheel Scammell draw bar tractor, an AEC Major eight wheeler, an ERF artic and a second hand

Sentinel DG8 on solids ex Baxters of Newcastle upon Tyne.

All went well for the company after the war and they joined forces with other haulage contractors into a holding company called Hauliers Ltd. In 1948 they disappeared into the Nationalised road services with general haulage vehicles going into the BRS and heavy haulage vehicles going into the British Transport Commission Heavy section later called Pickfords.

In 1946 the firms three Fowlers were sold off No. 17106 to Stephen Mustill of Neston No. 10318 to Walker Denton of Hyde No. 17293 to J. Puddifer of Liverpool.

101. — E. Box 100 tonner with 120 ton excavator passing through Liverpool.

46. – J. Burrow & Sons of Leigh, Malvern, Worcestershire class B5 Fowler No. 9421 of 1902 "The Malvern Queen
en route from Bury to Nailsworth Glos. with a rotary mill. 1902.

104. — H. Viney of Preston Leyland steam wagon and trailer which operated the first balanced trunk service between
Liverpool and Blackburn with change over point at Longton, south of Preston, approximately 1906.

E.W. RUDD, London

E.W. Rudd began trading at 16 Page Street in Westminster just prior to 1890. Realising that his base was in the wrong area to promote bulk movements, Rudd decided to move to Bow in the heart of the East End which was the centre of the engineering, shipbuilding and dock related industries.

With the coming of steam road vehicles Rudd was on friendly terms with Frank Garrett of Leiston the traction engine and wagon builder. This was very unusual because Garrett did not normally mix his business and private lives. Rudd contributed ideas to the design of the first Garrett overtype wagon which was delivered to him in 1909.

The wagons he purchased were Coulthards, then a Foden followed by a fleet of Garretts. The main customer who contributed steady work for his growing fleet was a frozen meat importer shipping carcasses from New Zealand and South America. Rudd delivered the meat to cold stores and Smithfield meat market from the docks.

Messrs. Fraser & Chalmers, Boilermakers with their works next door to Rudd's depot remained faithful customers. A B6 Fowler No. 14921 of 1917 was purchased to deliver their products to the docks using a steel-wheeled boiler bogie.

Rudd achieved some notoriety in the dock strike of 1904 when he led a convoy of wagons through the striking dockers picket line riding on the first wagon.

When Scammell Lorries Ltd., of Watford started producing their famous articulated six and eight wheelers, he bought one of the first and continued using them until nationalised in 1948.

In April 1933 E.W. Rudd loaded a 120 ton transformer from Hackbridge of Walton on Thames for transportation to Barking Power Station in Essex. Using a Crane built double swan-necked trailer with eight double-tyred solid rubber wheels at both ends below a full turning lock which could either be towed with a Vee bar or locked in a straight position this was a very modern trailer for that period and one which could be towed from either end.

Unfortunately he had only one big Fowler and hired two of Hickey's Burrells to assist, No. 3489 "City of London" for tracing and the crane engine No. 3829 "His Majesty" to backshove and hold back. The load was too heavy to travel over the river bridges and they were forced to convey it by river. The transformer was delivered to Greenland Dock on the Southside of the Thames where the Port of London Authority's 200 ton floating crane (the world's largest) lifted the transformer onto a barge. It travelled by river to the Royal Albert Dock and the crane lifted it back on to the road vehicle, by which it was conveyed to Barking.

The third transformer was lifted in March 1936 using Coulsons of Park Royal Fowler No. 9964 instead of one of Hickeys Burrells which was on other work. With Coulson tracing Rudd and Hickey behind braking they stopped before descending a hill at Cobham to apply the trailer brakes. When moving off Rudds started before Coulson, causing Coulson to slew across the road into the ditch taking Rudd with it. The two Fowlers ended up on their nearsides lying in the ditch while the trailer remained on the road. There have been many theories on how this accident happened but this is the truth of the matter.

111. — E.W. Rudd of Bow London. Garrett wagon with trailer hauling tank No. 27720 of 1909.

112. — E.W. Rudd petrol driven chaindrive wonder, 45 ton Scammell of the 20's with verticle tank.

113. — E.W. Rudd 1920's 45 ton Scammell with Scammell built trailer moving a condensor.

114. — E.W. Rudd same outfit with 30 ton transformer.

115. — E.W. Rudd with 1930's built petrol Scammell loaded with 45 ton transformer for Canada.

It took three days to salvage the two engines, Rudds appeared to have survived without any faults but Coulsons suffered a bent crankshaft (and to this day the flywheel has a slight twist on it) and was towed away.

Hickeys Burrell came from behind as tracing vehicle and a Scammell became backshover. This transformer went to St. Katherines Dock just below Tower Bridge before being transferred to the barge to sail it over to the Royal Albert Dock as the previous transformers.

E.W. Rudd were the main contractors for the movement of the Hackbridge transformers to Barking Power Station. Marstons Road Services of Liverpool moved the first in 1932 on the 100 tonner but it may have been Rudd that sub-contracted it to them. Sometimes this happened in heavy haulage when a big trailer was tied up with another customer.

The heavy haulage side of the business continued to grow using the 45 ton Scammell articulated unit as

116. — E.W. Rudd petrol Scammell with 40 ton transformer. 1930's.

117. — E.W. Rudd Fowler No. 14921 Reg. No. HR 4634 using Scammell trailer with forecarriage carrying a crane cabin passing through Ipswich.

118. — E.W. Rudd with 90 ton transformer from Hackbridge of Walton-on-Thames for delivery to Barking Brothers Power Station hauled by Coulsons Fowler No. 9904 Reg. MT 2340 of 1904, Rudd's Fowler No. 14921 Reg. HR 4634 and back shoving Hickey's Burrell No. 3489 Reg. PB 9624 ''City of London'' plus Rudds Scammell following. E.W. Rudd's name was placed on all engines and trailers working for Rudd. The trailer looks as if it belongs to the electricity authority of that area. This was common practice in England and Wales but not in Scotland. In an emergency the Power Company only required motive units to haul the trailer. 14th March, 1936.

119. — E.W. Rudd Fowler No. 14921 in a ditch along with Coulsons Fowler between Hersham and Cobham Surrey, on the Seven Hills Road. This was a regular occurance before airbrakes operated from the tractor. The loaded trailer kicked the two leading engines off the road. Coulsons Fowler had to be towed back to Park Royal with a bent crankshaft. 14th March, 1936.

a tractor with a ballast box mounted above the turntable. Using a tractor at the front of the trailer and another at the rear they moved numerous big loads. On the general haulage side they supplied a large number of contract vehicles painted in the customers own colours.

In 1948 on Nationalisation, the meat haulage section went into the BRS meat section, general haulage into the BRS and the heavy haulage into Pickfords colours.

120. — E.W. Rudd. Another view of the ditched engine. They would have some job removing the coupling pin before winching the Fowler out. Two days were lost removing the engines and preparing to continue the movement.

121. — E.W. Rudd Fowler at end of Kingston By-pass awaiting police escort to travel into St. Catherines Dock on the south side of the Thames where the transformer was lifted by a floating crane on to a barge for transit to the East India Dock on the north side of the Thames where it was reloaded on to the trailer for delivery to Barking. This was because it was thought that none of Thames bridges could carry this weight. 17th March, 1936.

122. — E.W. Rudd Fowler traced by Hickeys Burrell No. 3489 backshoved by Rudds Scammell. (There goes another clutch plate). The number plate behind the tradeplate belongs to Hickeys "Black Prince" No. PE 8171 instead of PB 9624

123. — E.W. Rudd Fowler with the "City of London" No. 3489 and "Black Prince" No. 2701 both Hickey owned Burrells with the Electricity trailer which has straight carrying beams fitted instead of the previous cranked frame. At least three of those transformers were supplied for Barking, MRS moved one, this could have been the second with the unlucky third.

PICKFORDS

Pickfords started in the eighteenth century with a string of pack horses delivering goods in and around London. With the coming of the railways they set up a delivery and pick up service for the railway companies in London and the Home Counties. They also expanded into furniture removal and packing for overseas shipment as well as throughout the British Isles. When steam wagons appeared two Hindley of Dorset steamers were required to carry goods across London. In the early 1920's Hays Wharff Cartage bought them over.

After the amalgamation of the many small railway companies into the big four — The London Midland & Scottish Railway, The London North Eastern Railway, The Great Western Railway, and the Southern Railway, each put up an equal amount of money taking over Hays Wharff completely and using it to buy over other haulage companies.

The history is only interested in the heavy haulage of Pickfords side and not the parcels or furniture removal divisions, although Pickford's first traction engines were mainly used by the furniture side which had pick up vans being transferred by crane engines.

Pickford operated several steam tractors and road locomotives in the London area on various movements.

133. — Pickfords London. This is the original firm not the nationalised Pickfords. Burrell 8NHP single crank compound road locomotive No. 2430 of 1901 and two Aveling and Porter tractors. 1906.

134. — Pickford Ltd., with same Burrell in London Docks. 1907.

135. — Pickfords, Ltd., Fowler class R3 (7NHP) crane locomotive No. 12749 "Daisy" Reg. No. XC 9654 of 1911 moving railway container 1936.

136. — N.E. Box Manchester Fowler "Titan" B6 road locomotive No. 14843 Reg No. NC 2021 of 1919 hauling a 30 ton electric generator casing in Manchester on a Fowler trailer 1921 later to join Pickfords.

137. — Pickfords just after purchase of N.E. Box Fowlers "Jix" No. **16264** Reg. No. NF 2032 and No. 17105 Reg. No. VM 2110 "Atlas" with Fowler 80 ton trailer. 1930/1.

138. — Pickford "Atlas" with transformer on Eagle trailer. Early 1930's.

139. — Pickfords Fowler "Titan" No. 14843 with steam accumulator from Cochranes of Annan to Bradford Dyers Assoc., on 32 wheeled Dyson/Crane trailer. 11/4/1932.

140. — Pickfords Fowler "Talisman" No. 16263 Reg. No. NE 2834 with 32 wheeled trailer delivering 80 ton transformer to the South of Scotland Hydro Scheme.

141. — Pickford Fowlers No. **14344** "Vulcan" Reg. No. NC 2022 and No. **17105** "Atlas" Reg. No. VM 2110 hauling 90 ton Ferranti transformer on the 32 wheeled Dyson/Crane trailer followed behind by Road Engines and Kerr (Haulage) Ltd., Burrell "Clyde" Reg. No. GA 7818 to assist them into the delivery point and winch off the transformer to place it in working position thus allowing the two Fowlers to return for the next job Newton on Ayr. 1938.

142. — Pickford showing rear view of trailer with packing timber for unloading and front of "Clyde".

143. — Pickford 100 ton trailer being built at Teesside Bridge & Engineering Co. 1932.

144. — Pickfords 100 ton Scammell with large shearing machine Reg. No. BLH 21 complete with 20 mph speed plate it never travelled at 20 mph in its life, 5 mph was nearer it. This was the second 100 tonner built.

145. — Pickfords McLaren/Fowler "Rover" started as steam McLaren 8NHP No. 1570 of 1918 was sent to Fowlers in the middle 30's to have a diesel fitted. Known as the "Haunted House" because of the queer noises and antics of the machine. As no brakes were added it was nearly impossible to stop it. One points police-man in Manchester held all the traffic up then disappeared behind a tramcar until it passed.

146. — Pickfords petrol Scammell with 1917 tank going to scrap. 1930's.

147. — Pickfords sixwheeler with unusual load. 1946.

One of the first Pickfords buy outs was of The London Traction Haulage Co. Ltd., first registered in March 1899 to take over the business of Henry Cattermole & Son. They had new a 10 NHP Fowler No. 7523 of 1896. Second hand in 1898 Fowler No. 4748 of 1894 Class B. New in 1900 Fowler No. 8843 Class B.

After the new company was set up they purchased an Aveling & Porter second hand in 1899 No. 1912 of 1883 an 8NHP single crank. New Fowler No. 12749 of 1911 an R3 crane Reg. No. XC 9654 later to have Pickfords No. 829. Ex War department Fowler No. 14115 of 1914 a B6 Reg. No. XC 9653, Pickfords No. 828.

71. — London Traction Haulage Co. Ltd., Class B6 Fowler No. 14115 Reg. No. XC 9653 "The Lion" new 1914. Moving a team excavator on its own tracks.

72. — London Traction 'The Lion' with 72 feet long x 9ft diameter, 32 tons on two steelwheeled bogies.

73. — London Traction with class R3 crane Fowler No. 12749 Reg. No. XC 9654 new 1911 with an H beam on double trailers. Bought by Pickfords London.

Coupe Brothers of Sheffield was also among the first to be taken over by Pickford also in the 1920s. Coupe took over J.D. Robinson also of Sheffield in 1913 who had a Fowler No. 8634 of 1899 Class B4 Reg. No.WA 3605 new to Robinson also another Fowler No. 6927 and Aveling Porter No. 2952. Coupe bought a new Garrett tractor No. 32631, Reg. No. BJ 2395 in 1914 which lasted into Pickfords.

109. — Coupe Bros. Sheffield two Fowlers No. 6927 and No. 8634 leading Aveling Porter No. 2952 hauling 80 tons ex Brightside Foundry.

110. — Coupe Bros. Sheffield 112 ton casting hauled by five engines, the two Fowlers plus unknown could have been a hire plus Aveling and Garrett tractor No. 32631 of 1914 Reg. No. BJ 2395. Late 1920's.

In 1930 Norman E. Box of Manchester offered his heavy haulage business to Pickford. Mr. J.N. Drummond Pickfords heavy haulage supremo agreed price and conditions. On the 15th March 1930 the firm became Pickfords with NEB managing for 5 years. The fleet included 8 NHP McLaren No. 1570 'Rover' 1918, B6 Fowler No. 14843 'Titan' 1919 Reg. No. NC 2021, a D5 Fowler No. 15785, Reg. NC 6022 'Ajax' 1922, B6 Fowler No. 16263 Reg. NE 2834 'Talisman' of 1925, B6 Fowler No. 16264 NF 2032 'Jix' of 1926, B6 Fowler No. 14844 'Vulcan' of 1916 with crane and crane B6 Fowler No. 17105 Reg. VM 2110 'Atlas' of 1928. Two 25 ton Scammells and a 45 tonner all fitted with petrol engines. Plus all the old trailers including the 85 ton double swan neck Fowler and the new Dyson/Crane 32 wheeled-trailer years before its time.

This was the last firm to be taken over for a few years to allow the fleet to become consolidated and make a bit of profit. All the Coupe Bros., vehicles had all to be replaced and new vehicles added to Manchester and Birmingham depots as well as new depots being opened in Leeds and Derby.

Two AEC's with low loading bodies were ordered, rigid eight-wheelers with a maximum gross weight of 22 tons and as they weighed approximately seven tons the vehicle could carry fourteen tons and were used to carry small transformers, switch gear etc.

McLaren 'Rover' was sent in to Fowlers to have the boiler, engine and top hamper stripped out and have a Fowler diesel engine and gearbox fitted. Nicknamed the "Haunted House" by drivers and crews as no additional brakes were fitted to replace the reverse gear. It refused to stop, just sailed on regardless of parking brakes.

In 1929 Scammell Lorries, Ltd., built three one hundred ton vehicles. One for Marston Road Services Ltd., one disappeared into South America and one registered BLH 21 was for a tin mining company in Cornwall and went to Garretts of Leiston to have a crusher etc., built on the trailer. This tractor turned up at Pickfords Manchester depot being used as a drawbar tractor with a 30 ton Eagle trailer. It was on hire from Scammell until the patent run out that Marston held on the trailer. When this happened Messrs. Crane built a trailer similar to Marstens but without the jockey wheels that cost Pickfords three times the tax of Marstons 100 tonner.

In 1941 Pickfords bought up Coulson of Park Royal London.

COULSON & CO.,
Park Royal, London

The firm moved from Brauncewell, Lincolnshire in the mid 1920s to London. From there they specialised in moving gravel pit barges and equipment as well as the general heavy haulage work of a city. They also undertook the moving and re-erection of machinery, with six steam wagons assisting Fowler B5 No. 9904 Reg. No. MT 2430 and various steam tractors.

In late 1929 MT 2430 arrived in Scotland to move two 75 ton transformers from Rannoch Station to the Power Station at Kinlochrannoch a distance of 12 miles assisted by a local owned hired Fowler. Each movement lasted three weeks as the wheels had to be plated for the whole distance owing to the road being built over moss.

In 1934 they arrived at Rannoch with three big Fowlers, the two additions were No. 14861 Reg. MH 5876 and No. 14871 Reg. YK 1046 but the loads still required about three weeks travelling time. They also moved a 75 ton transformer from Abernethy to Newburgh in Fife before returning home.

Pickfords took over in 1941 and it was only then that new tackle was purchased. Most heavy haulage firms were in similar straits through lack of cash.

105. — Coulson & Co. Ltd., Park Royal, London. Fowler No. 9904. MT 2430 "Alice" of 1901
at White City London with large beam.

106. — Coulson with "Alice" from the front.

107. – Coulson in Scotland 80 ton transformer 30th November 1934 from Rannoch Station to Kinlochrannoch Power Station.

108. – Coulson Fowler No. 14871 Reg. No. YK 1046 awaiting orders.

Here is a list of the steam vehicles owned by Coulsons:—

MT 2430 No. 9904 Class B5 of 1904 new to E.W. Wright of Alton Hants, sold to Coulson, 1929, bought by S. White (dealer) Owslebury, Hants, in 1943 and sold to K. Frost of Norfolk of preservation.

MH 5876 No. 14861 Class C Special or R3 ex W.D. Fowler, sold to Allen Knight & Co. Huddersfield in 1946 (cut up). YK 1046 No. 14871 Fowler ex WD via Foley of Bourne and Cole of Shepherds Bush both dealers, to the Challow Sawmill Co. of South Orney, Glos. Sold to W.G. Partridge of Walcut Wilts and in 1931 to Coulsons (cut up).

TRACTORS

FE 2561 (later CT 3974). Foster 14353, new August 1919 5 ton tractor. Later owned by W. Day of Thame, Oxon. Last licensed 1938 and believed exported.

FE 2872 (later CT 3975) Foster 14377, 5 ton tractor. Later owned by E.S. Spencer, Croxley Green, Herts, resold 1945 to Hacket of Croxley Green and resold 1946 to Oaklea Nurseries, Ltd., Radlett Herts.

WILLIAM KERR & CO.
Machinery Brokers, Mavisbank, Glasgow

In 1898 Wm. Kerr & Co. opened up in business at Mavisbank as machinery merchants and brokers and bought a second hand Burrell the following April No. 2988 of June 1898 an 8NHP named "Charlie" to haul and erect Lancashire boilers into working position for Penman of Dalmarnock, Glasgow.

The business was started by Thomas Currie Kerr using his fathers name as he was a foundry owner in Kilwinning, Ayrshire. T.C. Kerr already an expert on valuation and handling of machinery of all descriptions recognised the value of outside squads working with haulage engines when no other contractor supplied this service.

In 1904 he quoted for delivering water pipes up Snowdonia in Wales for Messrs. Bruce Peebles of Edinburgh as part of the Cwm Dyli Hydro Scheme. This job was carried out in 1905 and the power station was opened in 1906. Three engines were purchased for the job then sold at the end of it — no records are left of them.

1906 they took on an outside job in Portugal erecting steelwork and machinery for J. & P. Coats Mill at Quinta de Cravel, three miles from Oporto, moving to Brazil in 1908 and back to Portugal. In 1911 it was St. Petersburg in Russia then erecting steelwork for Selfridges building and the GPO in London.

Meanwhile the haulage side was advancing in leaps and bounds. Up to 1912 their work mainly was moving Lancashire and economy boilers for both Penman and Wilson of Lillybank Glasgow. No marine work was attempted until TC was approached by Messrs. Barclay Curle who had two boiler shops in

CT 4565 Garrett No. 33380 of 1918, 5 ton tractor ex WD sold to J. Hickey & Sons. Believed to be still in existance as Showland Tractor Ruston 52698 of 1919 SCD Tractor ex WD by 1926 with Chapman of Lenham Kent. Auctioned 6.9.26 to Ovenden of Sittingbourne Kent and by 1927 with Arnold & Son of Branbridges, Kent. CT 4143 Ruston 52754 of 1919 SCD tractor ex WD. Later with E.G. Dowell of Wimbledon, Surrey. Sold to E.L. Chipping of West Ewell in 1935 and cut up by 1938.

CT 4854 Garrett 33406 of 1918, 5 ton tractor ex WD. Sold to F. Honour of Amersham Bucks, cut up.

WAGONS

FE 1418 Clayton & Shuttleworth 47039 of 1914, 5 Tonner ex F.J. Pember of Harlesden Middlesex in 1924 scrapped 1930. FE 3965 Clayton & Shuttleworth of 1915 ex Sims Becket & Partners of Willesden Green in 1924, scrapped 1930.

M 9026 Foden 6464 of 1916, 5 Tonner 1927 ex P. Keevil of Paddington to scrap 1933.

MH 1043 Foden 11554 of 1924 6 tonner fitted with crane ex W.J. Boyes of Peckham London.

Glasgow, one in Kelvinhaugh Street and one in Govan at Whitefield Road where it was proposed to build 120 ton boilers for shipment. This was the reason another 10 NHP Burrell second hand arrived in January 1912 and "Clyde" came in October the same year.

The marine work had been carried out by The Road Steam Engine Co. of Finnieston who operated the Thomson Road Steamer and had done so since 1872. Also a small contractor McFarlane who used two Thomsons on this work.

Four Burrells were needed to haul the 120 ton boilers on four wheeled trailers with no turning lock. Charlie the 8NHP, "Lord Roberts" a 10NHP two speed No. 1997 of July 1897 purchased March 1903, the 10NHP No. 2105 of June 1898 purchased January 1912 and "Clyde" 12NHP No. 3419 of October 1912. If one Burrell was not available the Fowler B7 No. 11271 of October 1907 purchased new, was used.

Nothing else was purchased until 1914 when a three ton Foden wagon secondhand joined the fleet No. 2396 of December 1910 Reg. M 2687 last licensed 1928. Then an 8NHP Aveling & Porter No. 5012 of May 1902 joined in 1915. Four more Foden wagons came 1916. No. 5876 of March 1916, 5 Ton Reg. M 8456, No. 6070 of March 1916, 5 Ton Reg. M. 8458, No. 6140 of March 1916, 5 Ton Reg. M 8462. They all disappeared in 1919.

The outside erection squads were fitting out munition factories and placing boilers in as usual during hostilities. Another 5 Ton Foden arrived in February 1917 No. 6912 new Reg. M 9127 which lasted until December 1928.

148. — W. Kerr & Co., Mavisbank Glasgow single crank compound Burrell, Cwm Dyli Hydro electric scheme North Wales. Llanberis railway station was used as base stores by the main contractor Messrs. Bruce Peebles, Ltd., of Edinburgh. All the pipes came by rail, then by traction engine to the mountain, then loaded one at a time on to a narrow gauge railway and hauled up by stationary steam winch. 1905/6.

149. - W. Kerr & Co., steam winch in unhospitable countryside at the end of the line. 1905.

150. — W. Kerr & Co., even horses were used to haul the rail bogies. 1905.

151. — W. Kerr & Co., according to the Central Electricity Generating Board three traction engines were used on this haulage. Unfortunately only two photographs have turned up although the half of Wales have been looking for prints or information. H. & W.E. Hughes & Son were not involved in this operation although they were within forty miles at Llanwrst. Burrell hauling two trailers up the Llanberis pass. Loaded with timber and contractors tipping bogies — 1905.

Four McLarens were purchased from the War department in 1919. No. 595 of May 1897, 8NHP, No. 1594 of October 1917, 10NHP Reg. G. 6804 which lasted into 1943 then scrapped. No. 1600 of November 1917, 10NHP Reg. GA 7820 scrapped 1941. No. 1627 of July 1918, 10NHP Reg. GA 7821 scrapped 1942 worn out. Late 1920 a Foster crane engine No. 14189, 6NHP Reg. AG 4137 only lasted a few months.

Another job that Kerr had acquired was rail locomotive moving from the three factories of the North British Locomotive Co. Ltd., Hydepark and the Atlas in Springburn and Queens Park at Polmadie on the South Side of Glasgow. Using the fourwheeled boiler bogies the locomotives had a rough ride to the docks until T.C. Kerr designed and had built at P. & W. McLellan, Ltd., Glasgow the first heavy crank framed trailer in the world in 1926. With a thirty six foot bed behind the swan neck which had a double axle forecarriage and triple axles at the rear all mounted on iron wheels with no brakes fitted. The trailer weighed 36 tons and was nicknamed the "Loch Ness Monster".

In 1928 the last Foden wagon arrived as most of the previous ones were sold No. 7932 of March 1918 Reg. M 9605 5 Tons lasting until 1936. In 1930 the "Loch Ness Monster" had the iron wheels replaced with solid rubber-tyred wheels running in brass bushes. One set of wheels at the rear had to be taken off as the trailer refused to turn corners when loaded.

152. — The Chapel in the Valley. Cwm Dyli hydro scheme power station. 1905-88.

153. — W. Kerr & Co., 10NHP No. 1997 "Lord Roberts" Reg. No. GA 7816 two speed road locomotive of July 1897 and No. 2088 "Charlie" 8NHP road locomotive of June 1898 with Lancashire boiler to New Lanark cotton mills the road in is down a steep hill with a hairpin bend. Before 1914.

154. — The Gourock Ropework Co. Ltd., Leyland steamer to move the raw bales down and the finished goods up to the railway station in Lanark.

155. — W. Hamilton of Hurlford Ayrshire Foster crane No. 14189 Reg. No. AG 4137 6NHP new May 1920 in Kilmarnock with a statue of Sir James Shaw. This engine was owned by W. Kerr & Co., before being sold to Hurlford.

156. — W. Kerr & Co., Burrell's "Clyde" No. 3419 Reg. No. GA 7818, 12 NHP road locomotive and "Lord Roberts" No. 1997 Reg. No. GA 7816, 10 NHP road locomotive at St. Cuthberts Co-operative works in Bread Street Edinburgh delivering a marine type boiler into the works. On right of print Paddy Slavin "Clyde" driver for 20 years, before Watty Muir standing alongside him inherited the job, Watty drove "Lord Roberts" for approximately 15 years. Early 1920's. Those trailer wheels would make some mess of the Glasgow to Edinburgh road.

'157. — W. Kerr & Co., Burrell's "Clyde", "Lord Roberts", "Charlie", and Fowler No. 11271 of October 1907, B7. Hauling 100 tons boiler into Whitefield Road crane in Princes Dock. Middle 1920's.

158. — W. Kerr & Co., rear view of load.

159. — North British Locomotive Co. Ltd., using Rail to move narrow gauge locomotives to Clyde Villa crane
at Plantation Quay. 1920's.

160. — Road Engines & Kerr (Haulage) Ltd., Burrell "Clyde" after amalgamation of the firms. Transferring 25 ton transformers off rail wagons in Perth. 1933.

In 1926 other crank framed trailers were built for other work. Those also had rubbers fitted.

T.C. Kerr died in January 1932 leaving chaos behind him. With no funds to run the business, in the middle of a slump in business. Across the water at Finnieston, the Road Steam Engine Co., was no better off and McFarlane had closed the doors in 1929. Bob Kerr, T.C's brother called on the Road Steam Engine Co., and after negotiations decided to merge the Companies. Thus Road Engines & Kerr (Haulage) Ltd., came into being.

With all the Thomsons scrapped the two Avelings sold, a slimmed down organisation closing one office and two yards and paying off most of the Finnieston staff.

Two second hand petrol Scammells, one articulated and one tractor came in 1936 with another articulated a year later. In 1937 they were in cash trouble again when Wordie & Co., a railway contractor approached them with a view to buying the firm.

Six years after the merger Wordie became the new owner. When two second hand engines were bought a Fowler No. 9986 B5 of August 1904 Reg.

NL 1028 to replace the other Fowler and a McLaren No. 1650 of January 1919, 10NHP Reg. EB 4903 ex "Wharfdale Terrier".

Only two engines were to come, in 1942 the Fowler "Supreme" No. 20223 of March 1934, B6 Reg. EU 5313 and Burrell Simplicity No. 4092 of October 1930 8NHP Reg. EU 4429. They both were sold in 1951.

In 1905 T.C. Kerr bought a second-hand Foden No. 771, 7NHP built that year ex "The Thistle" keeping it only just over a year. It was too light for his work but it could have been used in place of "Charlie" possibly working in Wales.

When Wordie took over new diesels including Scammells, ERF's and a 50 ton Foden. Also new Dyson trailers two off 75 ton concentrated weight and 110 ton spreadover. 50 tons articulated low loaders and semi lowloaders.

When the Road Steam Engine Co., merged with Kerr they owned six Thomsons and an Aveling & Porter 8NHP road locomotive.

161. — Road Engines & Kerr Burrell "Clyde" with 20 ton water tube boiler ex Babcocks & Wilcox Ltd., Renfrew for shipment 1935.

162. — Road Engines & Kerr Burrell "Clyde" filling with water before leaving Vickers Armstrong. Scotswood Road, Newcastle upon Tyne with 50 ton weight diesel rail locomotive for India being shipped from Glasgow. 1936.

163. – Road Engines & Kerr petrol Scammell with new Dyson 45 ton trailer in Liverpool. 1937.

164. – Road Engines & Kerr ''Clyde'' and ''Lord Roberts'' with rudder post from Beardmores Parkhead Forge to R.M.S. ''Queen Elizabeth'' at J. Browns Clydebank. 1937.

168. — Road Engines & Kerr ERF taking a new 50 ton Dyson trailer home. 1939.

170. — Road Engines & Kerr Fowler "Supreme" No. 20223 Reg. No. EU 5313 rating B6 new March 1934 and Burrell "Simplicity" No. 4092 Reg. No. EU 4439 rating 8NHP although nearer 10NHP with Loch Ness Monster trailer built 1926 hauling 4-6-2 Malayan locomotive weighing approximately 70 tons down North Street that is now part of the M8 Glasgow. 1945.

171. — Road Engines & Kerr Burrell "Clyde" passing through the Glasgow Cross in all her glory with empty trailer bound for the N.B. Locomotive Co. Ltd., Springburn. 1946.

172. — Road Engines & Kerr "Supreme" hauling & "Simplicity" holding back down Castle Street with a Malayan locomotive for shipment July 1946.

173. — Road Engines & Kerr "Simplicity" and "Supreme" with an Egyptian locomotive in St. Vincent Street heading for Stobcross Crane. 1947.

183. — Road Engines & Kerr (Haulage) Ltd., McLaren G6804 No. 1594 of 1917, 10NHP with 50 ton sternframe casting from Beardmores of Parkhead Glasgow awaiting a lift at Finnieston steam crane for shipment to Harland & Wolff Ltd., Belfast. 1936 approximately.

184. — J. Young & Co., (Kelvinhaugh) Ltd., 200 ton crane about to lift fishing boat.

WORDIE & CO.
Buchanan Street, Glasgow.

Wordie & Co., was partly owned by the London Midland and Scottish Railway Co. Ltd. Wordie was chairman of the company which operated in excess of 3,000 horses mostly Clydesdales and a large fleet of motor vehicles by the late 1930's. From two stables and a garage in Glasgow, a large stable and garage in Leith and Aberdeen. Not much smaller in Dundee and Perth. Then various sizes in Stonehaven. Forfar, Montrose, Dumfries, Lockerbie, Stranraer, Stirling Denny, Brechin etc., in Scotland.

In Northumberland Wordie & Co., operated brown coloured vehicles before and after taking over Currie & Co., of Newcastle and Doncaster, also they either owned or partly owned Grococks of Sheffield.

In Ireland both North and South they operated out of railway goods yards. The familiar colours of dark blue and dark red, the same as the Scottish colours. Any visitor from Glasgow felt at home when in Belfast or Dublin on spying a Wordie vehicle where I believe they are still running.

Wordie owned seventeen steam wagons of various makes before buying motor vehicles, of course, they disappeared on nationalisation in 1948 except in Ireland.

New Steam wagons owned all five tons.

	Yorkshire	No. 114	July 1905	
	Yorkshire	No. 115	July 1905	
	Yorkshire	No. 124	Sept. 1905	4 for sale Oct. 1913
	Yorkshire	No. 128	Dec. 1905	
	Yorkshire	No. 132	Dec. 1905	
M 4598	Foden	No. 3482	Jan. 1913	last licenced Dec. 1933
M 5313	Foden	No. 3898	Aug. 1913	Scrapped 1926
M 5479	Foden	No. 3946	Oct. 1913	sold 1923 to J Craig of Glengarnock
KT 827	Aveling Porter	No. 8122	Nov. 1913	later with J. Wilmot, Showman
M 5855	Foden	No. 4246	Feb. 1914	Scrapped 1929
M 6748	Foden	No. 4710	July 1914	Scrapped 1929
M 7208	Foden	No 5184	Mar. 1915	Scrapped 1933
KT 7320	Aveling Porter	No. 8702	Jan. 1916	No trace
MA 1047	Foden	No. 8994	July 1919	Scrapped 1933
MA 3808	Foden	No. 10052	July 1920	Scrapped 1930
MA 3817	Foden	No. 10054	July 1920	Scrapped 1930
GE 7648	Foden	No. 13612	Dec. 1929	Put on pneumatics Aug 1933

165. — Road Engines & Kerr new 75 ton concentrated weight or 110 tons spread overall on trailer ex Dyson. 1937.

166. — Road Engines & Kerr McLaren No. 1594 on 1600 with 80 ton marine boiler ex D. Rowan on the Loch Ness Monster at Finnieston crane. 1938.

167. — Walter Muir R.E. & Kerr's leading driver from 1936 when he took over "Clyde" wearing his striped collar the engine drivers badge of office. 1941.

CURRIE & CO.
Newcastle upon Tyne

	New Fowler	No. 9182	B5 of 1902	Sold before 1921
	New Fowler	No. 14587	R3 of 1916	Reg. BB 4143
Second-hand	Fowler	No. 8473	B5 of 1900	Reg. NL 1559 ex Bland of Gasforth

Currie ran three 45 ton Scammells at Newcastle and one at Doncaster.

NATIONALISATION OF TRANSPORT 1948

The railways and general haulage companies were nationalised in 1948 into a number of separate groups. The railway companies became British Rail. General haulage vehicles went into a group called British Road Services. But . . . the railways also owned a huge road haulage fleet comprised of general haulage which also went into the BRS, meat haulage (by Hays Wharff and Garlic Burrell & Edwards) which went into the Meat Section of BRS and there was also a Tanker Section and a huge Heavy Haulage section. The heavy haulage and the tankers did not come within the scope of the Act. However, General Hauliers who also had a heavy haulage section, such as E.W. Rudd and E. Box Ltd., were nationalised and their heavy haulage taken into the Pickfords Group. This was the largest organisation and with all their depots and plant it was decided to save painting and reorganising simply to carry on the Pickford name and add the other companies to the fleet. In hindsight it was not a good idea as previously these firms had been competitors and many drivers had no love for Pickfords or their crews.

Wynn of Newport had a general haulage fleet as well as a large heavy haulage section. They decided to carry on in heavy haulage and then made it successfully. On the other hand John Young & Co. (Kelvinhaugh) Ltd., Glasgow, had four and sixwheelers to carry long and out-of-gauge loads which worked in conjunction with the low loaders. The four and six wheeled vehicles were nationalised but after two years the lowloading business had to be sold to the Board because it could not work on its own.

So Pickfords, they all became, with the British Transport Commission Lion on each side of the vehicles, except "Simplicity" and "Supreme" which did not have enough space on the side to put it. Overnight Road Engines and Kerr (Haulage) Ltd., became Pickfords main Scottish depot.

The depot carried on but now included as before new comers from Isaac Barrie along with their heavy plant.

Curries of Newcastle moved into a new heavy haulage depot at Birtley in Co. Durham, later to be joined by Siddle C. Cook's heavy section from Consett.

In theory it was a great idea, unfortunately with people the way they are, it did not work. It became a top heavy organisation with the top not knowing what the workers were doing.

Nationalisation lasted from 1948 to 1956, when the first of the groups were denationalised. This was the general haulage section which was gradually sold off to private owners. The last of the British Road Services section was the subject of a management buy-out by the staff and workers in the early eighties along with Pickfords heavy haulage and furniture sections and the former British Rail delivery vehicles.

So Pickford, today is the third separate company to bear this name.

174. – Pickford not the original, now nationalised into the Transport Commission but called Pickford. Scammell 100 tonner with diesel rail locomotive BLH 21 for shipment 1949.

175. — Pickford ex E. Box 100 ton Scammell with Australian locomotive at Hydepark Glasgow. 1950.

176. — Pickfords Fowler "Supreme" parked in R.E. & Kerr's yard before being sold with the driver James Hudson. 1951.

177. — Pickfords ex Box 100 ton Scammell on regular work moving locomotives to the docks in Glasgow 1953.

178. — Pickfords Birmingham base Diamond T with the 100 tonners artic trailer (BLH 21) using a forecarriage hauling a large transformer. 1955.

180. — Pickfords winching the trailer around the corner.

181. — Pickfords safely on to the road with Bob Whitlock in charge. 1966.